AN ALTERED SPIRIT

The Twelve Steps and Ebenezer Scrooge

Anna Fruehling

BALBOA.PRESS
A DIVISION OF HAY HOUSE

Balboa Press books may be ordered through booksellers or by contacting:

Balboa Press
A Division of Hay House
1663 Liberty Drive
Bloomington, IN 47403
www.balboapress.com
844-682-1282

Because of the dynamic nature of the Internet, any web addresses or
links contained in this book may have changed since publication and
may no longer be valid. The views expressed in this work are solely those
of the author and do not necessarily reflect the views of the publisher,
and the publisher hereby disclaims any responsibility for them.

The author of this book does not dispense medical advice or prescribe the use
of any technique as a form of treatment for physical, emotional, or medical
problems without the advice of a physician, either directly or indirectly. The
intent of the author is only to offer information of a general nature to help
you in your quest for emotional and spiritual well-being. In the event you use
any of the information in this book for yourself, which is your constitutional
right, the author and the publisher assume no responsibility for your actions.

Print information available on the last page.

ISBN: 978-1-9822-6680-6 (sc)
ISBN: 978-1-9822-6682-0 (hc)
ISBN: 978-1-9822-6681-3 (e)

Library of Congress Control Number: 2021907189

Balboa Press rev. date: 04/20/2021

Contents

Acknowledgments ix

Introduction.. xv

The Twelve-Step Call 1

Denial, Justification, and Rationalization or "Humbug"......... 1

Experience, Strength, and Hope.. 4

A Word about the Ghost... 10

An Observation on Self-Destruction 10

Marley's Insanity.. 13

Faith and Fear.. 14

A Power Greater Than 14

Fezziwig and His Ball 16

Character of a Higher Power... 18

GOD: Gift of Desperation or Good Orderly Direction........ 18

A Word to My Predecessors 19

When the Student is Ready, the Teacher Will Appear.......... 21

As We Understood Him 22

If You Do What You Did, You'll Get What You Got........... 22

If You Want to Be Different, Do Different 23

Scrooge Witnesses How His Actions Affect the Cratchits 25

Self-Deceit or Self-Awareness 52

For Members of Twelve-Step Fellowships............................. 63

For Mary Rose, my best friend—and
the bravest woman I know

Acknowledgments

I owe the writing of this book to the twelve steps Bill W.
formulated so many years ago. Without these principles as
a guiding force in my life, I would probably be dead from
an overdose, by my own hand, or at the very least a chronic
malcontent, hell-bent on self-destruction. The Twelve Steps
have altered my spirit. They continue to renew and infuse my
spirit with increasing hope, faith, truth, love, and many other
spiritual principles that make my life worth living regardless
of life's circumstances.

Right now, we are living in the time of COVID and
political unrest. Through the twelve traditions, addicts are
able to practice "principles before personalities." I believe the
best way to be of service to self, society, God, and others is to
do the inside job. Using the steps brings about a miracle in the
broken perception and spirit of suffering addicts. Part of the
miracle has to do with the fact that *we* work the steps. The steps
ought never be worked alone. The old saying "an addict alone
is in bad company" is true.

Addiction of any kind—including food, sex, work, drugs,

alcohol, or people—causes guilt and shame, which can cause us to isolate and alienate. The suffering of a junkie living on Skid Row may appear to be a higher price to pay for addiction than an obese woman hiding behind loose clothing, declining invitations to parties, and always wearing a mask of wit and humor to hide her struggle, but the feelings inside are familiar to both. Personally, I believe what my dear friend Bitten Jonsson says about addiction: "One disease, many outlets." Whatever your outlet, the twelve steps are the solution.

I would like to thank the mentors I have had over the years.

Julie L.

My first sponsor. She had six months clean when she agreed to sponsor me. She said things like, "There is no such thing as a using emergency; just because you feel like using, doesn't mean you have to!" Emergencies consisted of fires, car accidents, bleeding out, and other such dramatic events.

Having your feelings hurt was to be expected. Hurt feelings may feel like an emergency, but they aren't. She made it clear that I was responsible for my actions, regardless of how I felt. Her words ruminate in my subconscious mind endlessly:

- "No is a complete sentence."
- "It's normal for an addict to want to use; it shouldn't surprise you."

- "You are not the hub of the wheel. God is. You're a spoke—you just go around."

Thank you, Julie. The time you gave me is more appreciated and valued now than ever before. Your words of truth mixed with humor are priceless gifts that keep on giving.

Nell N.

My second sponsor. My friend. My heart.

I asked her to sponsor me when she had eighteen months clean. I had nine years. She didn't want to sponsor me, but I insisted. I told her I had been praying about it, and I knew she was "the one."

A few days later, I called her because it was the anniversary of my father's death, and I was feeling down. Nell began talking about her own father. She spoke about the sights and sounds of his barber shop. The smell of Barbicide, the sound of the clippers, the old men speaking Italian … my father was an Italian barber in San Francisco. Our memories could not possibly be more alike! By the way, if you don't have a higher power yet, feel free to pray to mine!

Nell would often say, "Do you know how much God loves you?"

At the time, I was struggling with self-loathing. Her words were a balm to my shattered spirit. Whenever I confessed to wanting to put my finger on the detonator button of whatever "circumstance" I had trouble accepting, she would say, "Why would you want to shit in your own nest, honey?"

Apparently, grown-up birds do not shit in their own nests! Pretty smart, actually.

Thank you, Nell. I'm pretty sure you and Mary are the only women on the planet who know me so well and love me for exactly who I am. I am so very grateful to have had the privilege of being your "sponsee" for so very many years.

Pam J.

My third and current sponsor. I asked her to sponsor me the day after Easter in 2014. I wasn't looking for a new sponsor, but when I heard her share about her journey with forgiveness, I was blown away. God stepped in. Pam lives in California, and I live in Nebraska. I asked someone if they knew how I could get her number, and she knew Pam's sponsor. She called someone who knew Pam's number and texted it to me. What a blessing!

My self-loathing is completely gone because of my relationship with this powerful woman:

- "Life is right now—this is it!"
- "There comes a time in every relationship where you just have to be OK with what it is."
- "Don't let anyone dim your light!"

The difference her perception has made on mine is night and day. The day after Robin Williams committed suicide, I confessed that even with years of abstinence from drugs, I still occasional struggled with thoughts of suicide. I told her I knew drugs weren't the answer.

She knew my story. She knew I "used to oblivion" in my active days. The goal was to disappear. My self-centered fear told me I was a waste of space. I had to shut that voice off in my soul. When we had that conversation, she had been sponsoring me for about four months. I can't say her exact words, but her confidence in my ability to be restored to sanity changed me forever. I am OK. I will be OK. The self-loathing was ripped out by the roots that day. I will never again decide how to feel about myself based on another person's opinion of me. I am free. "God don't make junk."

Thank you, Pam. I love you so much. Your love for me is palpable despite the distance that divides us. I have never been so free, so grown-up, or so responsible for my own self. There is a quote I like to reverse, which makes me think of you: "With great power comes great responsibility." I like it better this way: "With great responsibility comes great power." I tend my own spiritual garden today with the help of the Master Gardener (my HP), and you, Pam J.

Mike C.

Mike was Julie's sponsor, and he made it possible for me to believe in God. He always introduced himself the same way: "I have a God, and she's black."

My very first prayer was to a cast-iron Aunt Jemima bank I had because my ex was an antique dealer. She looked strong enough to come between me and using. Julie told me not to call her in the middle of the night if I wanted to use. She told me to pray instead. I said, "To what? I don't believe in God."

She said, "That's OK—God believes in you."

God believes in me? My mind was blown. That night, I wanted to use so bad that I could smell it. I thought of Mike's words and prayed to my bank. It was a sincere plea to be rescued. I felt a shift in my spirit that night. I have come to believe that God knows who God is—and God hears all prayers.

Mike, you helped me more than you will ever know. You cornered me after meetings and told me the truth with love so many times! It used to make me feel embarrassed and uncomfortable. I now know you weren't crawling up my ass for fun! You cared. I changed and grew because you chose to interfere with my diseased thinking. God bless you, sir. Wherever you are.

Thank you, Mike. There are no words.

Introduction

In my active addiction, I was hopeless, afraid, lonely, and ashamed. I isolated myself, hoping no one would figure out how worthless I was. I wrongly thought myself to be a "bad" person. "Only 'bad' people hurt others like I managed to do," a voice in my head repeated convincingly. Only "bad" people made the kind of mistakes I made. I truly believed my life was a mistake. I believed I should have never been born. I thought everyone would have been better off without me.

I desperately wanted to stop using and found I could not. No matter how hard I tried, I could not stay clean. My chronic self-pity, self-loathing, and self-centered fear drove me back to using every time. This endless loop of despair rendered me unable to get clean and stay clean for any length of time.

I was spiritually dead. Dead as a doornail. Had I actually been dead at the time, the mourners would most likely have been overheard saying things like, "Her poor children, "What a pity," "I, for one, am not surprised," "She didn't have a friend in the world," and so on. That is, if anyone bothered showing up for my funeral!

Let's take a look at someone we are all familiar with, someone who didn't know he was spiritually dead. Ebenezer Scrooge. Sound strange? I know. I've never been accused of being a regulation, status quo sort of person.

I don't want to talk about working the steps. I want to talk about *living* and *experiencing* the steps through the lens of *A Christmas Carol*, as written by Charles Dickens. This timeless tale has haunted me since I first began my recovery in a twelve-step fellowship on March 19, 1989. Someone at the meeting said, "Mistakes are temporary setbacks—not links in an unbreakable chain."

Right away, I had visions of Marley saying, "These are the chains I forged in life." That was it for me! I sat up a little straighter in my chair and leaned into the group to hear what was being shared.

I remain ever grateful for the lifesaving, life-giving, life-altering message my spirit began to hear that day. This short book is an expression of that gratitude.

Please indulge me as I compare the twelve steps with Charles Dickens's *A Christmas Carol* and its characters. I am hopeful that reading this will ignite your belief in—and passion for—the transforming power of the twelve steps and that you will come to believe that anyone can recover from anything. Anyone! From anything—if they are willing to embrace the spiritual living embodied in the steps and apply the spiritual principles to their own lives:

- "One is too many and a thousand never enough."
- "Mine occupies me constantly."

If you are an addict like me, you may understand the words of Dickens. Constantly, without ceasing, our thoughts are occupied by the desire to pursue our addiction to its bitter ends.

Obsession and compulsion fuel us to continue doing something harmful to ourselves and others, regardless of the consequences. Addiction is wanting to stop but repeatedly failing to keep your word to yourself. It is doing the same thing over and over again and expecting different results.

More. Different. Better. Whatever the person, place, or thing is, there will never be enough of it to "fix" me. We suffer from a *dis-ease*. I hyphenate the word to illustrate the discomfort we have living in our own skin.

Honestly, I don't believe it matters what your thing of choice is. If you "fixed" like I did—or Scrooge did—it might be a problem for you. Shopping? Sex? Dope? Work? Food? Does something occupy you constantly? Can we agree that this sums up addiction?

Scrooge was an addict. He thought only of money and was driven beyond his control by his impulse to have more.

In Disney's version of *A Christmas Carol,* Jim Carrey portrays Scrooge removing the coins off his dead partner's eyes as he lay in his casket. He had to have those coins! "Tuppence is tuppence," he gleefully says. "He got his fix that day. Two pennies' worth."

He wouldn't think another thought about his partner, Marley, for seven long years. He would continue fixing on his thing of choice for all of that time.

The Twelve-Step Call

Denial, Justification, and Rationalization or "Humbug"

"It's humbug still," said Scrooge. "I won't believe it."

The mention of Marley's funeral brings me back to the point I started from. There is no doubt that Marley was dead. This must be distinctly understood; otherwise, nothing wonderful can come from the story I am going to relate.

In this scene, Scrooge is about to be haunted by Marley. He is about to have the mother of all twelve-step calls!

***

"You don't believe in me?" the Ghost asked.

"I don't," said Scrooge.

"What evidence would you have of my reality beyond that of your own senses?"

"I don't know," said Scrooge.

"Why do you doubt your senses?"

Scrooge said, "Because a little thing affects them. A slight disorder of the stomach makes them cheats. You may be an undigested bit of beef, a blot of mustard, a crumb of cheese, a fragment of an undone potato. There's more of gravy than of grave about you, whatever you are!"

***

I could go on.

Dickens portrays Scrooge as a master of justification and rationalization who cannot—or will not—accept the reality of Marley's untimely visit. Instead, he manufactures a plausible excuse for what is happening.

This is common behavior for addicts. We manufacture enough bullshit to fertilize the world one hundred times over! We find it is easier than facing reality.

I totally understand Scrooge's response to Marley's visit. I have goose bumps as I think back to facing my own ghosts for the first time! I wanted to deny them. I wanted to be left alone.

Having someone else point out for us what we fail to see happening in our lives is terribly inconvenient, isn't it? Admitting powerlessness and unmanageability is inconvenient too. Our conscience pricks at us and we think, *it may be an undigested bit of…*

It challenges everything we think we know, especially who we think we are. We don't particularly like being "helped" in reaching the bottom.

Scrooge eventually asks Marley why he came.

***

"Mercy!" he said. "Dreadful apparition, why do you trouble me?" Scrooge wants to know why Marley wants to interfere with his using. Have you ever felt that way? "I'm doing just fine ... mind your own business."

"You are fettered," said Scrooge. "Tell me why."

***

This is my favorite part!

***

"I wear the chain I forged in life," replied the Ghost. "I made it link by link, yard by yard; I girded it of my own free will, and of my own free will, I wore it. Is its pattern strange to you?"

***

What an admission! Jacob Marley knows how to 'fess up. He took full responsibility for his chain, which sounds like some of the sponsors I've had.

Marley told Scrooge that he had been wearing a chain (presumably of his own making) that was as heavy and as long as his own some seven Christmas Eves ago. He let Scrooge know that he had been adding to it "link by link and yard by yard" since his own passing.

A Plea for Help

> "Jacob," he said. "Old Jacob Marley, tell me more. Speak comfort to me, Jacob!"

Experience, Strength, and Hope

Marley shares what he has learned with Scrooge. He shares his torment and his regrets. "I am here tonight to warn you that you have yet a chance and hope of escaping my fate."

According to Marley, a chance and a hope would consist of a visit from three ghosts.

Scrooge explains that he would rather not.

Nerve-racking! I can relate. Can you? Marley is brutal! Although, having faced my "ghosts," I would definitely encourage Scrooge to accept the visitors. In fact, if you have yet to face your own ghosts, demons, or apparitions, I encourage you to do this ASAP. Preferably you will do this with a Marley of your own, who has prior experience with facing ghosts and is willing and happy to share their experience, strength, and hope with you.

The Ghost said, "Without their visits, you cannot hope to shun the path I tread."

Scrooge pleads with Jacob to "take 'em all at once."

This always makes me laugh! Who wouldn't want to get it over with? There are many things I'd rather not do: go to meetings, get a sponsor, or work the steps. I always wanted the magic wand. You know, the quick, get-it-over-with cure-all?

I am told the steps are written in the order we should take them for a reason.

Have you been visited by any ghosts? Are you tired of forging chains? Want that upset tummy caused by denial to go away?

Me too…let's move on to step one.

Step 1: We admitted that we are powerless over our addiction, that our lives have become unmanageable.

***

"Seven years dead?" mused Scrooge. "And traveling all the time?"

"The whole time," said the Ghost. "No rest, no peace. Incessant torture of remorse."

***

Marley sounds pretty powerless, huh? He chased pretty, shiny things his whole life. Dying in active addiction leaves him in constant torment. He is filled with regret. He lost opportunities to love and be loved. His untreated addiction robbed him of the true pleasures of humanity.

I wonder what the ghosts of those we knew—those who died in active addiction—would want to say to us. Like Marley, they probably would implore us to be willing to change. I bet they would want us to know about the chance and hope Marley spoke of.

The Ghost said, "You will be haunted by three spirits."

Admitting we have a problem at all takes a lot of courage. It takes a little while for Scrooge to see that he has a problem. Oddly enough, we feel lightened by our admission. Honesty can have that effect. It seems to remove the weight of the mysterious burden we've been lugging around. Maybe it was the chains we forged all along.

An admission is only the first half of step one. We do our best to quit our "thing of choice" without any lasting success. We concede that we have "used" against our own will. We stop time and time again, but we can never *stay* stopped. Most of us understand powerlessness, but unmanageability is different.

> Light flashed up in the room upon the instant, and the curtains of his bed were drawn.
>
> "Are you the Spirit, sir, whose coming was foretold to me?" asked Scrooge.
>
> "I am."
>
> "Who and what are you?" Scrooge demanded.
>
> "I am the Ghost of Christmas Past."

"Long past?" inquired Scrooge.

"No. Your past."

The light of the Spirit disturbed Scrooge, and he had a great desire to cover the Spirit with its cap.

"What!" exclaimed the Ghost. "Would you so soon put out, with worldly hands, the light I give?"

Scrooge preferred the familiar darkness to the unfamiliar light. He feared looking at himself. He knew deep down that his own unmanageability had led to the heaviness of spirit he constantly felt and the realization that he had incessant regrets. He had buried himself in his work, his wealth, his gain. It made him feel powerful, and it protected him from intimacy. He didn't have to face his own feelings. In this way, he "fixed" his pain and sorrow, but all the money and power in the world wouldn't work for him any longer.

When Scrooge wondered what business brought the spirit, he was met with a direct answer. None of the spirits seem to be codependent in this story.

"Your welfare!" said the Ghost.

Scrooge thought a good night's sleep would be of greater benefit to him.

We always think we know best, don't we? In all honesty, what we knew about living brought us to our knees. I'm guessing this book isn't going to attract a lot of non-addicts. Just saying.

> The Spirit, sensing his thoughts, responded, "Your reclamation, then! Take heed!"
>
> Scrooge relented. He touched the Spirit's hand and was transported back.
>
> "He was conscience of a thousand odors floating in the air, each one connected with a thousand thoughts, and hopes, and joys, and cares long, long forgotten."
>
> "Your lip is trembling," said the Ghost. "And what is that upon your cheek?"

***

It is said that in addiction we lose our capacity to feel human. We also lose the ability to love and be loved.

"Strange to have forgotten it for so many years!" observed the Ghost.

Isn't it strange to have allowed the thing we "fixed" on to rob us of our joy and hope? Extinguishing the light with the cap?

At first, the thing we "fixed" on brings us relief. We love it, and we do it as often as we can. Soon, we lose the ability to stop doing it even when it no longer provides us with the relief it once did. We lie to do it, we cheat and steal to do it, and we torpedo relationships to do it. The promise of relief from our pain and emptiness calls us back like the Sirens in *The Odyssey*. We are powerless.

Now we are no longer doing the thing; the thing is doing us. We've lost our choice. We use no matter the cost. Our lives have become unmanageable.

Scrooge felt apart from. Isolated. Alienated. Alone.

He saw the "shadow of the things that have been" and felt pity for himself. Denial and self-pity kicked in.

***

"What was a merry Christmas to Scrooge? Out upon merry Christmas! What good had it ever done to him?"

They moved on to a large room full of desks.

At one of these a lonely boy was reading near a feeble fire; and Scrooge sat down upon a form and wept to see his poor forgotten self as he used to be.

***

He wept for his former self. Abandoned and forgotten as a child, he wept. For the child inside, the child that only wanted a merry Christmas.

But what was a merry Christmas to Scrooge?

A Word about the Ghost

I notice, in all the film portrayals of the first ghost, the spirit is always present for Scrooge. He allows him to feel. He does not judge or rush him. He never offers advice. He only offers his company and the comfort his presence brings. Sure, he asks a question or two—the kind of questions that cut to the chase. Scrooge is the only one with the answers to the questions. Good sponsors know that.

An Observation on Self-Destruction

Scrooge did not recognize how he was responsible for his own isolation as an adult. He withdrew from others, participating in no relationship outside of what was mandatory for him to run his business. Making merry was not for him. It was all "humbug."

"Christmas a humbug, uncle!" said Scrooge's nephew. "You don't mean that—I am sure?"

Scrooge had himself convinced he did not want to make merry. Most likely, it was easier for him to believe such a lie. He continued isolating and neglecting the child inside. It's often easier to reject someone first than to risk being rejected oneself.

Later in the story, he would not so graciously decline an invitation to spend the holiday with his nephew. Nothing will change his mind; his beloved little sister may have, but she died in childbirth. He is unable to give or receive love.

Stubbornness, self-deceit, self-loathing, displaced anger, self-centered fear, ego, and more lead addicts further into unmanageability.

In trying to manage his feelings, Scrooge managed himself out of so many good things in life! He refused to spend holidays with his sister's only son—what a way to pay homage to her!

His stinking thinking, his own misperceptions, led him to make the wrong choices in his life. He was too sick with addiction to know he even had choices. He was out of control.

Scrooge's life was unmanageable because he was a terrible manager! How have you been managing? Personally, I have found the need to get a new manager, a power greater than myself who could restore me to sanity…

Step 2: We came to believe that a power greater than ourselves could restore us to sanity.

***

"What idol has displaced you?" he rejoined.

"A golden one."

"This is the even handed dealing of the world!" he said.

"You fear the world too much," she answered gently. "All your other hopes have merged into the hope of being beyond the chance of its sordid reproach. I have seen your nobler aspirations fall off one by one, until the master-passion, Gain, engrosses you. Have I not?"

***

Wow! Give it up for Charles Dickens! The master-passion? It appears Scrooge already had a power greater than himself, and it could destroy him with insanity.

The capitol G in Gain is not a typo; Dickens intentionally capitalized the word. Brilliant!

Scrooge protests, and he asks her if he has changed.

She explains that he indeed had changed. "In a changed nature; in an altered spirit; in another atmosphere of life."

She releases him. Not that he tries convincing her to stay. He *is* living in "another atmosphere." Oblivious to this fact, Scrooge cannot be reached. His "master passion" has him by the balls!

Scrooge's "master passion," his obsession and compulsion, was a destructive power greater than himself. It drove him to insanity. It was the basis for every choice he made and every choice he forfeited making. Yes, I said *forfeited*. Choosing not to choose—as Scrooge did when he let his love walk away—is still a choice.

The insanity of addiction stems from this. We lose the ability to choose. We are victims of our own master passions. We bow down to a destructive power greater than ourselves.

Marley's Insanity

> As Scrooge looks out his window upon Marley's
> exit, he witnesses other chained apparitions
> unable to intervene for the good of humankind:
> "The misery with them all was, clearly, that
> they sought to intervene, for 'good' in human
> matters, and had lost the power forever."

***

Lost the power forever? This is exactly what Marley tried to convey to Scrooge. Marley had "lost the power forever." He did not wish the same fate on another. Knowing he had served the wrong power, his destructive master passion, and realizing the insanity of it, he desired restoration for Scrooge.

No one wishes to grow up to become an addict! Like frogs in a tepid pot of water, we are brought to a slow boil, unaware of the dangers that lie ahead. When the consequences of the disease become too great to ignore, we have the opportunity to repeat the same thing, over and over again, expecting different results or change.

Wouldn't it be nice to be restored? To live with dignity again—or maybe for the first time. To have no secrets to keep, no lies to manufacture, nothing to hide. To live a life without shame and guilt. To intervene for the good of others.

Faith and Fear

Just like Scrooge, most addicts "fear the world too much." We hide in our work, our drink, our dope, shopping, gambling, stuffing our faces, sexting, or cutting. We give up our values to our addictions until we no longer recognize ourselves. We become hopeless.

No one has the power to undo past mistakes. We can be restored today. We can start over right this instant. We can make new choices. We can let hope and faith become our guides instead of our all-consuming self-centered fear.

Replacing fear with faith requires assistance. Addicts alone will always be at risk of reverting back to our old thinking. My friend George always says that two are greater than one. That makes two addicts in recovery a higher power.

A Power Greater Than

If you have chosen to continue perusing through my musings, you will probably agree that we *had* been serving a greater power, a terribly cunning, baffling, and destructive force.

There are many things greater than ourselves. The ocean, a sunset, the twelve steps, unconditional love, gravity, politics, the seasons, illness, whether we were born good looking or ugly are all greater than us!

Step 2 states, "We came to believe that a power greater than ourselves could restore us to sanity," not *who* could restore us to sanity. This is not "God shopping" time.

If you practice a faith, great! If you don't have a practice, that's just fine. We begin with ourselves. We start with where we are and move forward. There is no need to compare one person's beliefs to another. Recovery is an inside job. All any of us needs to know is that we should strongly consider the nature of our higher power. No matter where we begin, we need a power that is loving and caring.

I never prayed any prayer besides this one: "God, if you get me out of this jam, I promise ..." I was never able to honor my promise.

My first sponsor was a barber and mother of four. She informed me that it was normal for an addict to want to use, and she assured me this was not an emergency. She told me just because I felt like using didn't mean I had to. She further informed me that I should not call her in the middle of the night over such a matter. She had the audacity to suggest I pray.

I responded, aghast, "To what? I don't believe in God!"

She said, "That's OK—God believes in you!"

I didn't know what to say to that. I was stunned and speechless.

In meetings, Mike C. always said, "I have a God—and she's black!" He never spoke at a meeting without making that entirely clear to the rest of us. He made it perfectly clear that each member had a right to his or her own understanding of a higher power.

Later that night, I felt the obsession to use creeping up on me, but I couldn't call Julie. It was too late.

I looked up at my mantel and saw her: my salvation, my higher power. There she stood, hands placed firmly on her hips, her painted-on white eyes penetrating my soul. She looked as though she was as confident and sure of herself—just as I was fearful and unsure of myself. She was a treasured antique I had bought at a rummage sale. A cast-iron Aunt Jemima bank. I bowed my head and prayed, "Aunt Jemima, please help me! I want to stay clean so bad! I'm so confused. If I really want to stop, why do I feel like using!"

The moment the words left my lips, a seismic shift occurred in my spirit. I believe it was my first encounter with the spiritual principle of humility.

Fezziwig and His Ball

The first ghost brought to mind his old boss, Fezziwig, under whom he had apprenticed. Scrooge lost himself as he gleefully watched his former self cheerily set up and enjoy Fezziwig's annual Christmas party.

Dickens said, "In they all came, anyhow and everyhow."

Everyone was welcome at Fezziwig's ball: the cook, the milkman, a boy who was suspected of not having enough because of his stingy master, a girl who was abused by her mistress, colleagues, neighbors, and friends gathered together, one and all, to celebrate!

It was similar to the rooms of twelve-step programs. It was a motley crew, but everyone was welcome.

Scrooge was completely immersed in reliving this joyful time.

***

"A small matter," said the Ghost, "to make these silly folks so full of gratitude."

"Small!" echoed Scrooge.

***

The spirit drew his attention toward his former self and his fellow apprentice, singing the praises of Fezziwig:

***

"Why! Is it not? He has spent but a few pounds of your mortal money: three or four perhaps. Is that so much that it deserves this praise?"

"It isn't that, Spirit. He has the power to render us happy or unhappy; to make our service light or burdensome; a pleasure or a toil. Say that lies in words and looks; in things so slight that it is impossible to count 'em up: what

then? The happiness he gives, is quite as great as
if it cost a fortune."

Character of a Higher Power

In this simple paragraph, written almost two centuries ago,
Dickens captures the qualities of a loving power, a power that
could choose to be punitive and judgmental but does not. It
really is the small things that give great meaning to life.

We all have this power in us, a God-seeking GPS, if you
will. In active addiction, most of us tarry along like Scrooge,
leaving a wide berth of destruction behind us.

Scrooge thought of his own clerk, and the power he had
over his "burden and toil." He wished he could say something
to Bob Cratchit just then.

Scrooge was finally aware. He was awake for the first time
in ages! His "god of Gain" had been his GPS, his guide to
living. Remembering Fezziwig's simple kind ways, Scrooge
was acutely aware that Fezzy served a far superior higher power
than Gain.

GOD: Gift of Desperation or Good Orderly Direction

Coming into "the rooms" for the first time, I was so warmly
welcomed that I was in a state of disbelief—maybe even a
bit suspicious. I met a lot of Fezziwigs that day. People were

celebrating life, being grateful, and sharing freely out of that gratitude. I felt a warmth and cheer I had forgotten existed. I believe I was truly welcomed. It was as if they had prepared for my arrival, expecting my visit all along.

Remember Scrooge's other atmosphere of life? Addicts live there too. But there is another atmosphere: the atmosphere of recovery.

Twelve-step group members *do* prepare for the arrival of suffering addicts! They create an atmosphere of recovery where all are welcomed. Just like Fezziwig's ball!

This welcoming atmosphere and the Fezziwigs at these meetings became a power greater than me. I had found something loving, caring, and greater than myself! I knew I was safe in that "atmosphere." People encouraged me to "do the next right thing" (sanity), to "keep coming back," and "not to pick up, no matter what!" If they could do it, so could I, they assured me.

A Word to My Predecessors

Thank you. Thank you for having the coffee ready for me. The happiness you have given "is quite as great as if it had cost a fortune."

I have been clean for thirty-two years as of this writing. Pinch me. Those dear old Fezziwigs from long ago were right about me! I could do it! So, can you. It's time to make a decision.

Step 3: We made a decision to turn our will and our lives over to the care of God as we understood Him.

"But though Scrooge pressed down with all his force, he could not hide the light: which streamed from under it, an unbroken flood upon the ground."

This step requires humility and willingness, but those qualities were unfamiliar to Scrooge. He desperately tried to extinguish the Ghost of Christmas Past with his own cap! The light that had illuminated his insanity would not be extinguished—not even by the absence of the ghost himself.

Once you have seen the light, it's impossible to unsee it.

The last words the first ghost spoke to Scrooge before his cap was forced upon his head were these: "I told you these were shadows of the things that have been. That they are what they are, do not blame me!"

No codependency here. This ghost must have had a black belt in Al-Anon!

I am eternally amazed at Dickens's insight. It had to be born of a power greater than himself! He was a mere thirty-two at the publishing of *A Christmas Carol*.

Scrooge could blame no one for the wreckage of his past. It was of his own doing, forged link by link as Marley had made clear to him.

When the Student is Ready, the Teacher Will Appear

Addicts think we know how to run the show. Scrooge controlled the amount of coal placed on the hearth! He knew his financial worth to the penny!

Making this decision means admitting we—addicts and Scrooge—know absolutely nothing about living life on life's terms. After all, what we knew about living brought us to the bitter ends.

This is when we "turn over control." We start doing the next right thing and leave the outcome to our higher power. We begin asking for help. Our minds are open to the idea that a better way exists, and someone else might know it.

***

"Spirit," said Scrooge submissively, "conduct me where you will. I went forth last night on compulsion, and I learnt a lesson, which is working now. Tonight, if you have ought to teach me, let me profit by it."

***

Without a hint of arrogance, Scrooge makes a decision to ask for help. His journey with the first ghost helped him clearly accept his predicament. He wants help. His help comes in the form of the Ghost of Christmas Present. This guy lives in the moment—hence the title. My personal favorite of the spirits, he helps Scrooge see where he has been "shitting in his own nest" as one of my previous spirits, I mean sponsors, Nelle, is fond of quipping! We will be seeing more of him, I assure you!

As We Understood Him

We are talking about a personal relationship here. No one can tell you what your understanding is. Mine grows and changes daily. Try allowing yourself to be cared for. Most people in meetings have a great deal of empathy for the still-suffering addict. Share honestly at a meeting. Yes, I am asking you to be vulnerable. What do you have to lose?

People at meetings strongly identify with each other through sharing. This response creates a connection to something greater than one addict. This community of recovering people is something greater than "me." As my friend George always says, "Two are greater than one." I agree.

If You Do What You Did, You'll Get What You Got

Nothing changes if nothing changes. No one can force our will. We don't have to do anything we don't want to do. If we like, we can continue on as if we never saw the light. We can be as stubborn and miserable as we choose to be. Many addicts do this for some time. Some old-timers call it "analysis paralysis," which happens to people who overthink themselves into a corner.

This really goes back to fear and expectations. Addicts really are a bunch of pussies. We will lie, cheat, steal, connive, manipulate, and put ourselves in imminent danger just to get the next fix. Will we ask someone for help? Hell no! *What if they find out what a piece of shit I am and reject me?* Come on. They gave you their phone number and told you to call them! They want to help, to be of service. They had help. They are looking to throw some bread back on the water, that was so freely given to them.

If You Want to Be Different, Do Different

The point of this step is to be willing to take suggestions and be willing to do something different. Willingness allows us to change our perceptions about the world in which we live. It helps us live in the present reality and recover inventively. We try out new ideas and behaviors with a hopeful new vision for the future. Willingness gives us the opportunity to start each day new—each moment new if we like. Willingness is an underlying eagerness that motivates us to write a new story about ourselves, a story in which mistakes don't terrify us and fear doesn't control us, one in which we can start over anytime we choose. We decide! Our disease no longer makes decisions for us. Some say that step three is the first real decision we make in recovery.

It's important to know what our disease sounds like and how it speaks to us and romances us. It wants us back. I call my disease K-FUCK radio. It has a major advertising budget, selling more, different, better, 24/7. Whenever it tunes in, and I hear it playing a few of the golden oldies from my using days, "What Does it Matter," "Why Should I," "Poor Me, I Can't," "Yeah, But," and my personal favorite, "I know," I envision myself changing the station. We can do that, you know? The first step said we were powerless over our addiction—not helpless!

Just because a thought enters our minds doesn't mean we have to act on it. My friend Julio often says, "Just because a bird lands on your head, it doesn't mean you have to let it build a nest there." Take this decision-making shit and run with it! Don't let the disease continue to be your higher power that calls all the shots.

We now have the three best tools necessary to continue our recovery: honesty, open-mindedness, and willingness.

It's time to take an inventory.

Step 4: We made a searching and fearless moral inventory of ourselves.

"You fear the world too much," she answered gently.

Scrooge's fiancé calls bullshit. Step 4 calls bullshit. It helps cut through the confusion and contradiction in our lives. It helps us begin living in integrity to our values rather than running on impulse.

If you are feeling nervous about step 4, you must be normal. I have yet to meet an addict who had no fear about working this step for the first time. We fear the world too much. We seem to honestly believe we are the worst person living on the face of the planet. We can't write an inventory about ourselves! We have second thoughts about this whole step-taking business. Maybe it's not for us.

Listen, we took a lot of risks out there while using. We went to the dope man's house, lied to loved ones about our activities, stole to support our habits, made promises we couldn't keep, and so on. We kept lowering the bar. "I'll stop shopping—after I use up my rewards." "Just one more look at the porn—and then I will be done forever." Every time we lowered the bar, we degraded ourselves more and more. We were trapped in our endless loops of obsession and compulsion.

Step 4 is a get out of jail free card. This step helps to free us from our self-made prisons. We expose the lies we manufactured for ourselves, which keep us stuck in our self-destructive patterns of living. We must take a good look at our patterns of behavior; otherwise, we are doomed to repeat them. Patterns are a problem.

Scrooge Witnesses How His Actions Affect the Cratchits

As they watched the Cratchits preparing for the return of Bob and Tiny Tim, Scrooge observed that Mrs. Cratchit was "dressed out but poorly in a twice-turned gown." Her daughter was dressed in worn-out garb as well.

Have you ever made a careless, thoughtless comment and later wished you hadn't? Welcome to the club. None of us walks through life unmarred by self-centeredness.

Bob came in with "at least three feet of comforter exclusive of fringe, hanging down before him; and his threadbare cloths dressed up and brushed, to look seasonable; and Tiny Tim upon his shoulder. Alas for Tiny Tim, he bore a little crutch, and his limbs in an iron frame!"

Scrooge watched as Bob shared how Tiny Tim hoped people would benefit by seeing him, hoping all who saw him would remember "who made lame beggars walk and blind men see."

Ebenezer never heard a complaint out of any of them. They enjoyed and made the best out of the very little they possessed. They had each other, and that was quite sufficient. In fact, it was quite a bit more than Mr. Scrooge possessed.

Finding himself interested in Tiny Tim's welfare, Scrooge asks the spirit about his chances. The spirit blandly states the truth: "If these shadows remain unaltered by the future, the child will die."

Scrooge pleads with the spirit to spare the boy.

The spirit offers a refresher course for those who suffer from amnesia: "If he be like to die, he had better do it, and decrease the surplus population."

Scrooge hung his head to hear his own words quoted by the spirit and was overcome with penitence and grief.

The ghost warns Scrooge to be careful about sanctimoniously passing judgment on what and where the surplus is: "It may be in the sight of heaven that you are more worthless and less fit to live than millions like this poor man's child."

At this point, Bob raises a glass to Scrooge and says, "The founder of the feast."

His wife does not initially join him in blessing Mr. Scrooge, but she relents for the sake of her beloved.

Scrooge heard, with regret, his own callous words more than once that night.

This is part of taking a fearless moral inventory. He showed "a courage not his own" as we say in the rooms. We must see the harm our addiction caused.

He had a growing awareness of the destructive patterns that had kept him imprisoned in a web of self-centeredness, fear, and isolation. With the sheets pulled back and his behavior exposed, he now had the chance and hope needed to escape the fate that Marley had warned him about.

The addicts in the rooms said, "Face everything and recover!"

I wanted an eraser when I got to the rooms. Instead, I got a nice sharp pencil and a fresh sheet of paper on which to pivot my story. I could change the ending. I could do something different. I could write a hopeful new chapter. I could start fresh.

Through the power of working the steps as suggested, I found out I didn't need to erase my past. I needed to accept it, learn from it, and write a new story in which my words don't always come back to haunt me. Today is a new day and another opportunity to live a life without incessant remorse!

Step 5: We admitted to God, to ourselves, and to another human being the exact nature of our wrongs.

> "There are some upon this earth of yours," returned the Spirit, "who lay claim to know us, and do their deeds of passion, pride, ill-will, hatred, envy, bigotry and selfishness in our name, who are strange to us and all our kith and kin, as if they had never lived. Remember that, and charge their doings on themselves, not us."

In this step, we charge our doings on ourselves. We admit the exact nature of our wrongs. No more blaming people, places, things, or circumstances for our predicaments. Our consequences are a direct result of our behaviors.

Many of us object to this confession. We may have blamed God for the mess our active addiction made of our lives. We can't fathom trusting another human being with our secrets— and haven't we already fessed up to ourselves?

The purpose of making an admission to God, ourselves, and another human being is about relationship. It is not about humiliation. We admit—and tell the truth—about the exact nature of our wrongs. The exact nature is not the same as the "inventory." The exact nature is about the brokenness behind the "inventory." Brokenness is the feeling we don't deserve to be whole and happy. It is the reason behind how we have been living. We stop hiding from ourselves, God, and other human beings to receive love and acceptance. We expose ourselves; we get naked and raw in this step. We learn to experience our full selves, not some imposter, mask-wearing, approval-seeking imitation of ourselves. The hurting unit has acted out of fear. It was afraid that we would never get what we want and need— and that we will never get what we want and need. Never mind that we really don't have a clue as to what that is!

***

In easy state upon this couch, there sat a jolly Giant, glorious to see; who bore a glowing torch, in shape not unlike the Plenty's horn, and held it up, high up, to shed its light on Scrooge, as he came peeping round the door.

"Come in!" exclaimed the Ghost. "Come in! and know me better, man!"

***

The spirit employs Scrooge too "look upon me. You have never seen the likes of me!"

These are the statements of a being who knows who they are. This is a person who is unafraid about being "known." This is the child of a good, kind Creator. This is someone who knows their own worth and values the worth of others.

See the real me. Take it or leave it. Love me or despise

me—but please see the real me. Unless I am fully known, I will never be fully loved. Masks and deceptions cannot be loved. They are illusions. In this step, we destroy the illusions. We admit our fears, our weaknesses, our strengths, our hopes, and our dreams to the three aforementioned entities. We become known.

The spirit transports Scrooge to many places during their time together. They haunt the markets, watch people gather to attend Christmas services, peek in on men working in a lighthouse singing carols, and all the while, the ghost is generously sprinkling blessings on any poor soul he encounters.

When they arrive at Bob Cratchit's home, the ghost blesses the little home with a broad grin and a sprinkle.

Scrooge is learning the nature of God. He wants to bless us! He is loving and caring. We can tell him anything. He wants to be with us. God knows us. Telling our higher power about our fears, desires, disappointments, anger, and despair—all of it—is about a relationship and communication. It is not a confession.

Scrooge witnessed all manner of humanity keeping Christmas that night. He was acutely aware that he had not kept the holiday himself in eons. Good and bad men kept Christmas alike, but Scrooge did not. He could see that now:

> "Ha, ha! Ha, ha … ha, ha!"
> "He said Christmas was a humbug, as I live!"
> cried Scrooge's nephew. "He believed it too!"

"More shame for him, Fred!" said Scrooge's niece, indignantly.

***

Fred points out that "his offenses carry their own punishment." Yes, they do! Our offenses hurt us most of all.

***

"I have no patience with him," observed Scrooge's niece.

"Oh, I have!" said Scrooge's nephew. "I am sorry for him; I couldn't be angry if I tried. Who suffers by his ill whims! Himself, always."

"I was only going to say," said Scrooge's nephew. "That the consequence of his taking a dislike to us, is, as I think, that he loses some pleasant moments that could do him no harm."

This good man says he means to give his uncle a chance at a merry Christmas every year! He will not give up on him. His faith in the chance of a miracle is great!

***

Tell another human being like Fred the exact nature of your wrongs. All my sponsors have been like Fred: patient, hopeful, kind, humble, and very aware that "but for the grace of God."

The mercy Scrooge received by eavesdropping on his nephew's conversation lightened his burden of guilt and shame. His nephew understood Scrooge's dilemma. This is how it feels to be truly known, exposed, and naked.

Scrooge had fallen into some bad habits because he feared the world too much. Fear is self-perpetuating. It carries an insidious power to regenerate itself into endless loops of mind-fucking thoughts. These loops (K-FUCK radio) make it difficult to come clean about ourselves. This is where the faith we gained in restoration in step 2 comes in handy. Tell on yourself. Don't wait for the fear to abate. Once you speak honestly of it to another addict, the fear will abate on its own. You are braver than you think. Don't be a pussy now. 'Fess up.

The spirit and Scrooge stayed and watched his nephew's party. Scrooge was getting so caught up in the fun and games that he often cried out answers to riddles as if he could be heard:

> The Ghost was greatly pleased to find him in this mood, and looked upon him with such favor.

OK, I'm tearing up right now! And looked upon him with such favor? I thought God wanted me to burn in hell. I couldn't have been more mistaken. I found out that God cares for me, others care for me, and I could learn to care for myself.

God and his servants here on earth are in the

blessing-sprinkling business. Allow yourself to get sprinkled. "Come and know me better" is the beckoning call of step 5.

Now we are ready to have our defects removed.

Step 6: We were entirely ready to have God remove all these defects of character.

***

"Ghost of the Future!" he exclaimed, "I fear you more than any spectre I have seen. But as I know your purpose is to do me good, and as I hope to live to be another man from what I was, I am prepared to bear you company, and do it with a thankful heart."

***

Scrooge knew he had served his "master passion," Gain, for far too long. He now realised the effect his stinginess and greed had, had on himself and others.

His supernatural visitors had helped him see the truth. The Ghost of Christmas Past shed light on him. The Ghost of Christmas Present helped him hope for a better way to live his life: free and "unfettered" by the chains he had forged thus far.

Hope was new to Scrooge, and he was somewhat frightened of it. He knew it meant being changed. He had been robbing himself—and others in so much as he could—of making merry for almost his entire adult life. Could he be changed?

We often hang onto our old ways of living and coping—out of a perverse familiarity. Many come from generations of brokenness and have never had a spiritual way of life demonstrated to them. Alternately, many come from good homes and find themselves in the grips of active addiction, despite their fine upbringings. The disease could give less than a fuck about the details. Addiction truly has no bias. Its victims come from all walks of life. We feel a sense of futility. *Maybe we made a mistake*, we think. *This twelve-step stuff just isn't my cup of tea.*

A cup of tea might steady your nerves. I remember thinking I needed to somehow become perfect, yet I was fully aware that perfection is unattainable! My first sponsor noticed how comfortable I was with the familiar and said, "How does it feel in that nice warm pile of shit?" She was letting me know that staying frozen in place and not moving forward would ensure that I would stay stuck. Warm and comfortable in my pile, preferring the familiar to change, I knew staying stuck wasn't the solution.

I had to ask myself if I really wanted to continue doing the same thing over and over again, expecting different results. No! Hell no! I told myself I could change. "I" was the operative word here. Oops, I had forgotten that I was a bad manager and that my life had become unmanageable. Honestly, I was so confused about this step and what it meant that I complicated the fuck out of it!

I understand now that the only thing I bring to this step

is the willingness to be transformed. I am open to letting God remove all these character defects. I become entirely ready to be changed. This readiness is ripe with hope, faith, patience, and tolerance. Trust your higher power. God loves fixing broken people.

Remember how the Ghost of Christmas Past came for Scrooge's welfare? God doesn't want us to pay for our mistakes. He wants us to pray for his help.

We are ready. Like Scrooge, we have "learnt a lesson which is working now." We remain open-minded and grateful. We see tangible evidence of our changing nature in our thoughts and deeds.

We are changing. We have placed our feet on the path they should tread. We become more confident. We practice humility as we accept ourselves as we are at this moment. Progress—not perfection—as they say!

Scrooge was ready to live free of the chains of loneliness, pain, and sorrow that his defects had inflicted on himself and others. He felt lighter. Hope had brought a glimpse of his new life into view.

Can you imagine a life without chains? I know many addicts who feel that this step was the true beginning of freedom for them. I am in complete agreement. By charging our doings on ourselves, we become willing to be changed. There is no more hiding behind a mask of character defects! We take baby steps into a new way of life. We stop believing the lies that manifested our self-centered fears into actions that brought destruction, and we begin to see our true natures emerge, unfettered by the chains of the past.

Step 7: We humbly asked Him to remove our shortcomings.

> "Is it a foot or a claw?"
>> It was two children, a boy and girl.
>> Frightful, hideous and miserable.
>> Yellow, meager, ragged, scowling, wolfish;
> but prostrate, too, in their humility.
>> "Spirit! Are they yours?"

***

No. The spirit explained they belong to us; they belong to humanity. He said they cling to him, appealing to their fathers (us).

***

> "Have they no refuge or resource?" cried Scrooge.
> "Are there no prisons?" said the Spirit, turning on him the last time with his own words. "Are there no workhouses?"

***

This is why we need to have our shortcomings removed. They hurt people. They hurt everyone around us. A shortcoming will always have ramifications—just as a pebble tossed into the water creates ripples.

Have your children had to walk around on eggshells? Have they apologized for breathing because you acted out on a character defect? Has someone gone without food or shelter because you needed the money for your fix? Has anyone ever felt frightened of you or intimidated by you?

Scrooge had become entirely ready. He knew it was his only chance for restoration. He had come to believe that a power greater than himself could restore him to sanity. He had made a decision to let God be in the driver's seat. He had taken inventory, admitted the exact nature of his wrongs, and become ready to have his defects removed.

Phew! Don't chicken out now! A lot of courage, perseverance, and hard work got you this far. Keep going! A little humility never hurt anyone.

> The children under the hem of the Spirit's gown had names, the boy, "Ignorance," the girl, "Want." The Ghost warned Scrooge to beware of them both …but most of all beware this boy, for on his brow which is written, Doom, unless the writing be erased.

Why? Why did the ghost so adamantly warn against ignorance and the lack of knowledge? Because being unaware is dangerous. When we don't see the wake of destruction we caused, we don't see the need for change.

Once, when I was about twenty, I decided to thoroughly clean my house. I began with the toilet. I started with bleach and added a bit of ammonia for good measure—and the fumes knocked me on my ass! My lungs closed up like a jail cell door. This is a humorous example of the dangers of ignorance, but only because I survived.

The girl Want is deficiency—being without essential things—and not about greed or desire. We as addicts are deficient. We lack some essentials. You could say we are anemic at life! We are vitamin deficient at people skills! Spiritually bankrupt! Our demeanor keeps everyone at a distance. We ensure our own isolation.

Dickens describes Scrooge as totally unapproachable. Children would not ask him the time, and no one would ask him directions:

> Even the blind man's dog appeared to him now;
> and when they saw him coming on, would tug
> their owners into doorways, and up courts,
> and then would wag their tails as though they
> said, "No eye at all is better than an evil eye,
> darkmaster!"

But who was avoiding whom? Really? Were you anything like Scrooge?

> But what did Scrooge care? It was the very thing he liked. To edge his way along the crowded paths of life, warning all human sympathy to keep its distance.

Ignorance leads to strange behavior. We don't realize we suffer from "want." … We deny ourselves the essentials—love, companionship, care, and kindness—by ignoring our need for them. After all, ignorance is bliss! We cannot want what we do not acknowledge. We put up false bravado. We convince ourselves we don't want or need these beautiful things in our lives. We push them away. We are the strange creatures under the robe.

The third ghost terrified me long before I read the actual book! I remember seeing the dark figure in the 1938 version of the film as if it were yesterday. It was so spooky. He was ominously cloaked in black, and a bony, crooked finger was his only form of communication:

> "When did he die?" enquired another.
> "Last night I believe."

The phantom had led Scrooge to a street-corner conversation. The men would go on to wonder about the departed's money. One noted it had not been left to him. They had a good laugh over that! One said he would not mind attending the funeral—if lunch were provided!

Scrooge was familiar with all these men. Scrooge knew the ghost was trying to teach him something:

> He resolved to treasure up every word he heard,
> and everything he saw, and especially to observe
> the shadow of himself when it appeared, for
> he had an expectation that the conduct of his
> future self would give him the clue he missed,
> and would render the solution of these riddles
> easy.

Though Scrooge diligently searched for his future self, his own image would not appear:

> Scrooge had heard a lot of talk about this man
> gasping out his last there, alone by himself.
> "Spirit!" said Scrooge, shuddering from head
> to foot. "I see. I see. The case of this unhappy
> man might be my own. My life tends that way
> now. Merciful Heaven, what is this?"

He was viewing a corpse loosely covered with a sheet.

> He lay in the dark empty house, with not a
> man, a woman, or a child to say he was kind to
> me in this or that.

"Let me see some tenderness connected with a death," said Scrooge, "or that dark chamber, Spirit, which we left just now will be forever present to me."

The Ghost of Christmas Yet-to-Come showed Scrooge his own clerk mourning Tiny Tim: "My little, little child!" cried Bob, "My little child."

He witnessed the Cratchit family bolstering each other's spirits. They would not feel sorry for themselves, only sorrow for their loss. They were grateful to have been blessed with Tiny Tim.

"Before I draw nearer to that stone to which you point," said Scrooge, "answer me one question. Are these the shadows of things that will be or are they the shadow of things that may be, only?"

Scrooge now understood a basic spiritual principle: if you do what you did, you will get what you got.

"Spirit," he cried, tight clutching at his robe, "Hear me! I am not the man I was."

Scrooge implored the spirit and humbled himself:

"Your nature intercedes for me, and pities me. Assure me that I may yet change these shadows you have shown me, by an altered life."

Scrooge accepts mercy for himself. He is willing to be altered by a power that is greater than himself.

Ready to face everything and recover (FEAR)? Have a pen and paper handy. You will be making a list. Don't forget to include yourself on it.

Step 8: We made a list of all persons we had harmed, and became willing to make amends to them all.

> "They are not torn down!" cried Scrooge, folding one of his bed-curtains in his arms, "They are not torn down, rings and all. They are here—I am here—the shadows of the things that would have been may be dispelled. They will be. I know they will!"

This means all persons—not just those we care about. This list should include the clerk at the grocery store, the librarian, your mommy and daddy, your significant other, kids—your own and the little runts down the street—teachers, politicians, clergy, aerobics instructors, bosses, and underlings.

Scrooge, like many of us with self-centered views of the world, hurt, frightened, and insulted everyone he met (sometimes without uttering a word). He underpaid his clerk, who could barely afford to keep his family on his meager pay. When Bob was able to make merry in spite of his circumstances, Scrooge replied, "My clerk, with fifteen shillings a week and a

family, talking about a Merry Christmas. I'll retire to Bedlam."
He then accused Bob Cratchit of picking his pocket every
December 25.

Two gentlemen approached him with a plea to help the less
fortunate, and Scrooge replied, "Are there no prisons?"

> A boy, stooping at Scrooge's keyhole, to regale
> him with a Christmas Carol. "God Rest Ye…"
> Scrooge grabbed a ruler with such an energy
> of action that the singer fled in terror.

What would happen if we all made "some slight provision
for the poor and destitute?" Would we need so many prisons?
Would we need so many foster homes? Would we need so many
group homes for troubled teens?

> The gentleman said, "Hundreds of thousands
> are in want of common comforts."
> Scrooge replies, "I wish to be left alone."

This is just a small smattering of those he has harmed and
owes amends to.

Make a list! Make a long, long list! Put yourself on the top
of the list. We harm ourselves most of all.

> The Spirit of Christmas Yet-to-Come points
> his bony finger at a headstone. The kind hand
> trembled.

Dickens describes it as a kind hand, and it was. The spirit was issuing a warning. The warning would be the final blast through Scrooge's denial. It would give him the chance and hope of escape Marley had spoken of.

Scrooge saw his name etched on the stone:

> "I will honor Christmas with all my heart, and try to keep it all the year. I will live in the Past, Present and the Future. The Spirits of all Three strive in me. I will not shut out the lessons they teach. Oh, tell me that I may sponge away the writing on this stone!"

Scrooge held up his hands in a prayer to have his fate reversed! All rationalization and justification for his actions were gone. He knew he was guilty of harming others! He was finally willing to take full responsibility for the harm he had caused.

Those nasty, old, rusty chains of guilt and shame would not survive in the light of truth and humility! Things get really different now! Let's join Scrooge for his ninth step.

Step 9: We made direct amends to such people wherever possible, except when to do so would injure them or others.

> Yes! And the bedpost was his own. The bed was his own, the room was his own. Best and happiest of all, the Time before him was his own, to make amends in!

"O, Jacob Marley! Heaven and Christmastime be praised for this! I say it on my knees, old Jacob, on my knees!"

Imagine if we all woke up excited about making amends, chomping at the bit to begin! Our recovery is a living amends. When we grow spiritually, we naturally amend our behaviors. What if we woke up feeling enthusiastic about having the opportunity to do so? I want this verve for life for myself. I think I will have a sign made to hang above my bed: "Best and happiest of all, the time is before me to make amends."

The other steps come first for a reason.

Many self-centered addicts want to be forgiven, and they think that making an apology after a short period of abstinence will suffice as an amends. These addicts self-centeredly declare, "Look at me! I stopped doing what I was doing so you can forgive me now!" They forget that what they were doing was only a symptom of their addiction. Stopping only allows recovery to become possible. It is, not in and of itself, recovery by a long shot.

Scrooge worked the steps in the order they were written and was rewarded by humbly regretting his past self-indulgent behaviors and the effects they had on him and those around him. He, to the best of his ability, would live differently today. He alone was responsible for his actions, and his amends did not place the unrealistic expectation that he would receive forgiveness from anyone. That is the epitome of doing the right thing for the right reason, completely absent of arrogance and self-centeredness.

So desperate to be changed in nature, Scrooge wept violently after his dealings with the last phantom. His regret was real. His whole being was transformed: "I am as light as a feather."

He is grateful for his recovery or his "reclamation" as the first spirit had put it. He goes on and on, telling himself, "Here is where Marley entered" and "Here is where the Spirit of Christmas Present sat."

Dickens said it was a splendid laugh:

> It's alright, it's all true, it all happened. Ha, ha, ha!
> The father of a long, long line of brilliant laughs!

Seeing things as they really are—and no longer as the way his self-deceit perceived them to be—he was able to accept his humanity. In that spirit he sets about making amends.

The first thought he had was of the Cratchits. Seeing Bob as a loving father, doing his best to care for his large family and ailing son, had changed Scrooge's perception of the situation. He saw that he himself was the guilty party, paying cheerful, hardworking Cratchit a pittance and then accusing him of being a "pickpocket." He would set things right beginning that very day:

> Running to the window, he opened it and put
> out his head, "What's to-day?" cried Scrooge,
> calling downward to a boy in Sunday clothes.

"To-day!" replied the boy. "Why Christmas Day."

"It's Christmas Day!" said Scrooge to himself. "I haven't missed it. The Spirits have done it all in one night. They can do anything they like. Of course they can. Of course they can. Hallo, my fine fellow!"

Wow. Wow. Wow! Scrooge has so much faith in the things he cannot explain! It was amazing.

He butters the boy up to get him to purchase the prize Butterball turkey hanging in the poulter's window and deliver it to the Cratchit's home anonymously.

"I'll send it to Bob Cratchit's," whispered Scrooge, rubbing his hands and splitting with laugh. "He shan't know who sent it. It's twice the size of Tiny Tim!"

For this act of total humility, no thanks were needed. He was having a hoot making amends. There was not a trace of wrong motives in this act. He even rewarded the boy handsomely. Gain was no longer his higher power. Scrooge was experiencing freedom. No more forging chains for him!

Scrooge hit the streets running that morning. Clothed in his best, he regarded everyone with a delighted smile. He looked so irresistibly pleasant, in a word, that three or four good-humored fellows said, "Good morning, Sir! Merry Christmas to you!"

It was music to his newly opened ears!

Just then, he ran into the portly gentleman who had walked into his counting house the day before.

"Scrooge and Marley's, I believe?" It sent a pang across his heart to think how this old gentleman would look upon him when they met, but he knew what path lay straight before him, and he took it.

He took it. He took the path face everything and recover. Go, Scrooge! You are a beacon of hope!

Scrooge takes the kind man's hands into his own, saying he hopes he was successful yesterday. He even wishes him a Merry Christmas!

"Mr. Scrooge?"

"Yes," said Scrooge. "That is may my name, and I fear it may not be pleasant to you. Allow me to ask your pardon. And will you have the goodness," here Scrooge whispered in his ear.

"Lord bless me!" cried the gentleman.

"If you please," said Scrooge, "not a farthing less. A great many back payments are included in it, I assure you. Will you do me the favor?"

Scrooge implores the man to come and collect his due. He then thanks the man.

"Thankee," said Scrooge. "I am much obliged to you. I thank you fifty times. Bless you!"

It's incredible! Have more thorough amends been made? My heart is overcome by Dickens's ability to write such honest prose about the act of a humble amends. Scrooge is ecstatic over his opportunity to live his life differently. He is blessed. He is obliged. Amen, Brother Scrooge!

When I was in my active addiction, I did many things I am not proud of. The guilt and shame kept me self-centered. By the time I reached step 9, I was beginning to understand and have compassion for those I hurt. I don't have unrealistic demands about life today. I am grateful for my life, especially for the opportunity to live it differently!

One way I make "back payments" is to buy and give away toilet paper. Ladies, you might understand! While using, I would steal toilet paper from gas station bathrooms because I couldn't afford my addiction *and* toiletries. Today, they lock toilet paper up because of people like me! Anyway, I felt terrible about leaving the next person without this valuable resource. In my recovery, I have provided many rolls of toilet paper to addicts just getting a fresh start. This may seem silly to some, but to me, it is something I want to do. It is something I am blessed to do! The recipients of the toilet paper are doing me—and my recovery—a favor. Because of them, I can lead a life transformed, a life of dignity and purpose. I am no longer bound by my old patterns of living.

Scrooge maintained his natural smarminess in his amends to Bob Cratchit. After toying with him for a while, he sets Bob up for the worst, and then he says, "And therefore, I am about to raise your salary!"

Bob thought him worthy of a "straight-waistcoat."

I like this amends because before I worked the steps, I thought twelve-step programs were a cult. I thought they would turn me into some kind of Stepford wife, devoid of personality. I learned through experience that the steps helped me become more of the real me than I ever was.

Step 10: We continued to take personal inventory and when we were wrong promptly admitted it.

> He went to church, and walked about the streets, and watched people hurrying to and fro, and patted children on the head, and questioned beggars, and looked down into the kitchens of houses, and up to the windows, and found everything could yield him pleasure. He had never dreamed that any walk—anything— could give him so much happiness.

Where the heck did the man who was "solitary as an oyster" go? He was replaced with a grateful person who was interested in the welfare of others. He even questioned beggars! He now knew what it was to humble himself. To plead. To beg. Beggars were no longer "surplus population."

Now he had to do some maintenance to do to keep the skip in his step, the laughter in his life, and the kindness in his heart.

For me, step 10 is about taking the vital signs of recovery. It's like checking to see if someone has a temperature, a stomachache, a headache or feels lethargic. When I experience one of these symptoms, I know I need to take care of my recovery *now*! I need to call my sponsor, go to a meeting, write a gratitude list, or read my literature. I need to humble myself and do whatever it takes so my addiction won't become a cancer that metastasizes itself back into my life, destroying all the spiritual principles I have been living by.

This step is about living life alive and awake! Old habits and patterns are deeply ingrained traits. I must take note of the grace of being alive and free today. I must see where I have hung on to my old self-centeredness and self-loathing. I don't want to sleepwalk through life today. Awareness of reality keeps me going on this spiritual journey known as the twelve steps. I want to see my life clearly, truthfully, and with my eyes wide open. Step 10 keeps me in touch my blessings and transgressions. Looking at only one or the other is a mistake. We may beat ourselves up with this step or adopt a holier-than-thou attitude if its purpose is misunderstood.

Self-Deceit or Self-Awareness

All addicts, actually all people, are mostly addicted to their own thinking. This is the root of most of our problems. Our perception is so true and real to us that we actually believe most of the bullshit our thoughts manufacture!

How we think leads to how we behave. If I am so attached to my way of thinking, I am unable to be open to other ways of thinking. We hurt each other with the labels we use to describe each other—such as Scrooge's dehumanizing "surplus population" comment—and these labels allow us to justify mistreating others. Scrooge was at his best when he had the humility to see himself as a beggar in need and humble enough to accept help:

> "Why bless my soul," cried Fred. "What's that?"
> "It's I. Your Uncle Scrooge. I have come to
> dinner. Will you let me in, Fred?"

Will you let me in? This question is packed with so much more than asking to have dinner with him. It is a plea to join his nephew as "fellow passengers to the grave." Scrooge is asking to do life with his nephew. He is asking for a second chance. He is awake now. He is no longer sleepwalking through life. He did not say that he was sorry. He *demonstrated* it by showing up to participate in his nephew's life. It doesn't get more "direct" than that!

Traveling with the Ghost of Christmas Present, Scrooge

saw how he had recently harmed his nephew. He was prompt in making amends.

Step 11: We sought, through prayer and meditation, to improve our conscious contact with God as we understood him, praying only for knowledge of his will for us and the power to carry that out.

> "Good Spirit," he pursued, as down upon the ground he fell before it. "Your nature intercedes for me and pities me. Assure me that I yet may change these shadows you have shown me, by an altered life!"
> The kind hand trembled.

The Ghost of Christmas Yet to Come's hand trembled? Why? Was it symbolic of Scrooge's total surrender? Is it showing his faith that God's nature is good and will intercede on his behalf? The words Scrooge spoke touched the spirit who has wanted and waited for nothing less. God was with Scrooge through his suffering. God is not the aloof bystander I used to believe he was. God is with me. God suffers with me when I suffer now and God suffered with me when I suffered in the past. He is also with you:

> I will honor Christmas in my heart and try to keep it all the year. I will live in the Past, Present and Future. The Spirits of all Three will

strive within me. I will not shut out the lessons
they teach. Oh, tell me I may sponge away the
writing on this stone!

I'm going to begin at the end of this amazing declaration of
Scrooge's. With the writing on the stone part, he is literally
referring to his tombstone and simultaneously pleading to die
to his old self. He is saying all three will strive within him. This
is his will for us. He has learned from the spirits' visits, and he
vows to never shut out the lessons they teach. He said *teach,*
a present tense verb, which shows he is willing to improve his
conscious contact. He says he will honor Christmas in his heart
and try to keep it all the year. He believes he will be given the
"power to carry it out" because the spirits will intercede on his
behalf.

Dickens has Scrooge "holding up his hands in a last
prayer to have his fate reversed" as the phantom seemingly
exits the scene. I say *seemingly* because the phantom only left
after Scrooge says he will honor Christmas in his heart. The
spirits reside in his heart now. The heart is where our spirit is
awakened. God can do amazing things with a change of heart.

In order to appreciate Scrooge's altered state, let us take a
look back at a conversation he had with his nephew:

"Merry Christmas! Out upon Merry Christmas!
What's Christmastime to you but a time for
paying bills without money; a time for finding

yourself a year older, and not an hour richer; a
time for balancing your books and having every
item in 'em through a round dozen of months
presented dead against you? If I could work my
will," said Scrooge indignantly, "every idiot that
goes around with Merry Christmas on his lips
should be boiled with his own pudding, and
buried with a stake of holly through his heart,
he should!

Scrooge tells his nephew to keep Christmas his way—and he
will keep it his own.

When Fred points out that Scrooge doesn't keep it, Scrooge
says, "Let me leave it alone, then."

Why don't you tell us how you really feel about it, Ebenezer?

His nephew won't back down. He passionately states his
perception of the Holy Time:

"There are many things from which I might
have derived good by which I have not profited,
I dare say," returned the nephew, "Christmas
among the rest. But I have always thought of
Christmas-time, when it has come round-apart
from the veneration due to its sacred name
and origin, if anything belonging to it can
be apart from that—as a good time; a kind,
forgiving, charitable, pleasant time; the only

time I know of, in the long calendar of the year, when men and women seem by one consent to open their shut-up hearts freely, and to think of people below them as if they really were fellow passengers to the grave and not another race of creatures found on other journeys. And therefore, Uncle, though it has never put a scrap of gold or silver in my pocket, I believe it has done me good, and will do me good; and I say God bless it!"

Fred has the Christmas spirit, but his uncle doesn't even have a clue. Fred understands that spiritual riches are much more rewarding than temporal rewards like possesions.

Scrooge is now keeping Christmas and the spirits in his heart. We have witnessed his reformation! He has prayed. Dickens makes this clear. What about meditation?

As I was thinking about writing this chapter, it occurred to me that Scrooge was forced to be with his own conscious while traveling with the silent Phantom of Christmas Future. He was left looking at himself with this spirit who only waited for him to draw his own conclusions. He begged the spirit to tell him a way out, and the spirit only pointed to his tombstone. The tombstone made Scrooge think about how he wanted to live. He didn't fear death, but he feared the legacy he would be leaving if he continued living the way he was. Scrooge meditated on his life and found hope from a higher power whom he was sure would have mercy on him and intervene on his behalf. He had a spiritual awakening!

All addicts think we are victims of our disease, but we are actually volunteers. Denial keeps us burdened with the weight of our own forged chains. We are under the illusion that we don't need to change. Addiction is the only disease that tells us that we don't suffer from it! Until we have suffered enough, we stubbornly refuse to alter our perceptions. We cling to our thinking, to our own detriment. Until we stop denying the writing on the tombstone, we are in grave peril, refusing to be transformed.

When I first came to a twelve-step meeting, I saw people filled with light. These were hopeful people, joyful people, and I questioned what I saw. If they were addicts like me, how could this be true? I stuck around and learned it was true. Today, it is my truth as well. I took suggestions and continued to grow and change through step 11. I am free of my chains, and like Scrooge, "I am light as a feather."

The steps continue to do their work in me. I am free of the heavy burden of guilt and shame. I now notice the afflicted at meetings. The still-suffering addicts are weary and burdened in their chains. I feel hope for them. They have come to the right place: a twelve-step meeting. I think I must have looked like them when I attended my first meeting.

Grateful for our recoveries, we begin practicing step 12.

Step 12: Having had a spiritual awakening as a result of these steps, we tried to carry this message to addicts and practice these principles in all our affairs.

> I mean to give him the same chance every year, whether he likes it or not, for I pity him. He may rail at Christmas till he dies, but he can't help thinking better of it—I defy him—if he finds me going there in good temper, year after year, and saying, "Uncle Scrooge, how are you?"

This is the essence of carrying the message. We must carry the message regardless of the outcome. We must carry the message regardless of who we are carrying it to. We must show up at meetings in good spirits and continue doing the right thing for the right reason even when someone doesn't understand it. We must trust God for the outcome:

> Scrooge was better than his word. He did it all and infinitely more; and to Tiny Tim who did not die, he was a second father. He became as good a friend, as good a master, as good a man as the good old City knew, or any other good old city, town or borough in the good old world.

The steps do their work in us; we do not really work the steps. The steps are not information; they are transformation. When we approach them humbly, we are changed. Approaching them like a to-do list that we get to finish seems to dissolve the power they have to transform. We misunderstand them, and we think we have something to do with our own "reformation." What we did brought us to our knees. We are begging for help and humbly pleading for the merciful intervention of our higher power. Humility—in fact, the very attitude of a beggar—gets us on our spiritual journey than any applied or forced pressure. When I admit I know nothing about living, I am open to learning. When the student is ready, the teacher will appear.

Scrooge, once so arrogant and self-absorbed, had so awakened spiritually that he was unable to live the same way. Recovery is an inside job, and the work done in us shows up in our dealings with others. This is evidence of an awakening. Do not be discouraged when scoffers cannot believe it! Not everyone believes in spiritual awakenings! It might be too *woo-woo* for them.

> Some people laughed to see the alteration in him; but he let them laugh, and little heeded them, for he was wise enough to know that nothing ever happened on this globe, for good, at which some people did not have their fill of laughter at the outset; and knowing that such as these would be blind anyway, he thought it quite well that they should wrinkle up their eyes in grins, as have the malady in less attractive

forms. His own heart laughed and that was quite enough for him.

Dickens must have been divinely inspired to write such a statement. At not quite thirty-two years of age, he possessed more wisdom in his little finger than most of us possess in our whole beings at twice his age.

He refers to the doubters as people who have the "malady." He is referring to illness, sickness, and "dis-ease" of a spiritual nature. Scrooge does not let it diminish him. He has no doubt about his own reformation, salvation, and awakening of the spirit within. There is no need to feel offended. He is way too grateful, joyful, and loved to feel the need to punish anyone who behaves the way he used to behave. This is one of many "but for the grace of God" moments in Dickens's tale. The ability to be able to see things from this perspective helps us "carry the message" without a hint of superiority.

An old saying claims, "Garbage in, garbage out." My second sponsor, Nell, often reminded me that whatever I feed will grow. I am free today. I am free to feed gratitude, faith, hope, love, and open-mindedness. I am free to abstain from obsessive-compulsive thoughts that many refer to as "stinking thinking."

The spirits in the rooms and the spirit of my higher power reside in me now, and they have taught me a lesson that is doing its work. I will not shut out the lessons they teach.

He had no further intercourse with the Spirits, but he lived the total abstinence principle ever afterward; and it was always said of him, that he knew how to keep Christmas well, if any man alive possessed the knowledge. May that be truly said of you, and all of us! And so as Tiny Tim observed, God Bless us, everyone!

Abstinence from what? What do you need to abstain from in order to recover? I know I need to abstain from stinking thinking! It goes without saying that I must abstain from the "master passions" of my past.

What will be said of us? How will we keep Christmas? Personally, just for this day, I intend to "make merry" and "generously sprinkle blessings" to the best of my ability.

Ode to Marley

Marley made a great effort to warn Scrooge that he had a chance and hope of escaping his own fate.

Not to know that no space of regret can make amends for life's opportunities misused! Yet such was I! Oh! Such was I!

Mankind was my business. The common welfare was my business; charity, mercy, forbearance and benevolence were all my business.

Thank you, Charles Dickens. Thank you, Marley. Thank you, Bill W., for the twelve steps and for sharing them with us—and for sprinkling us with them!

Thank you, God.

> Scrooge asked the ghost of Christmas Present, "Is there a peculiar flavor in what you sprinkle from your torch?"
>
> "There is. My own."
>
> "Would it apply to any diner on this day?" asked Scrooge.
>
> "To any kindly given. To a poor one most."
>
> "Why to a poor one most?" asked Scrooge.
>
> "Because it needs it most."

Everyone has a "peculiar flavor," a God-given "peculiar flavor" of sprinkles, to share. Sprinkle away! Sprinkle with a glad heart all you who were once poor of spirit and have been awakened! God flavored each of our sprinkles differently for a reason. He has given us what we need to carry the message to those who are still suffering.

You are enough. Be authentic. Be true to yourself. Go now to love and be loved.

"God bless us, every one!"

For Members of Twelve-Step Fellowships

We say all are welcome. We say there is strength in diversity. We say principles before personalities. Then our fear (lack of faith) and ego (self-centeredness) kick in, and we find ourselves judging another suffering addict. We decide they don't share the right way, they swear too much, they dress oddly, they talk too loudly, or they smell funny, ad infinitum. We discount someone's share because they relapsed again. We stop listening because they cuss too much. We stop showing the unconditional love that was shown to us and saved our own asses when we got here. We are comfortable with the way things are. We become resistant to change. We don't want a new format; what was wrong with the old one anyway? In short, we become like Scrooge before our transformation.

All of us are at risk of this phenomenon. The pandemic has had fellowships scrambling and rising to the occasion to continue having regularly scheduled meetings. Many addicts have resisted this change. We often oppress or suppress what we fear. Fear is the enemy of faith. Fear doesn't help us; it harms us. Somehow, we lose faith in the same higher power that has seen us through this far, and we start to try to manage things for ourselves. We forget our primary purpose, we forget what we have in common, and we begin to see all the differences.

Twelve-Step groups are fellowships; they are not social clubs. This fact allows each person to belong regardless of perceived differences. No one can help what color their eyes are, what color skin they are born with, how deep their voice is, or whether they were born rich or poor, or even their sexual orientation; each person is powerless over these factors. We all share a great deal of DNA in common, but a few snips in the DNA chain make me uniquely me, and you uniquely you. I'll show you my fingerprints if you show me yours! We are, as I see it, special. We are not unique, but each one of us is special.

Mike C. used to say, "God don't make junk!" I believe this was Fezziwig's mantra. Come one, come all! I strive to be a Fezziwig. Fezziwig knew that we all share certain human qualities that are common to all: the need to belong, the desire to love and be loved, fear, struggle, joy, pain, longing, hurt, loss, and anger. None of these traits have a color, a sex, an age, a sexuality, or a political point of view. These are the qualities of the nature of humanity. They aren't loud or quiet, rich or poor, or fat or skinny; they just are. The outside packaging is really just window dressing. The mantra "principles before personalities" embodies this simple fact. Nell N. always told me to see and hear things with my heart not with my eyes and ears.

When I first got clean, I didn't really have much of a personality. My experiences led me to shut down, and I retreated out of fear. I literally felt apologetic for the space I took up. I was a wallflower. Today, I speak loudly at meetings. What happened? The twelve steps happened. People loving me until I learned to love myself happened. Faith replacing fear happened.

I didn't know. I didn't have a clue about the transformation that would occur—or that it would continue to occur in my life.

I speak loudly and clearly at meetings because of the message. The message was carried to me so freely and gratefully, and I don't want anyone to miss out on it. It's not about me; it's about the message. This is why this book is not about my story. Who cares about *my* story? I care about *our* story. I care about *our* journey.

Scrooge is a guy we can all relate to, yet we can't compare ourselves to him. He's not even real, yet he embodies all the best and worst of human nature. We can all relate to him on the level of feelings. This is identification. Identification is that sense of knowing we are alike and the feeling of finally finding our people. It is essential for recovering addicts. Newcomers suffer when they cannot identify with the group. That's why I wrote this book about Scrooge and not about me. My whole spirit is hopeful that a clear message is found throughout its pages. Anyone can recover from anything with another addict, meetings, and the twelve steps.

I will continue to speak loudly at meetings. I will sponsor women and be sponsored. I will attend meetings regularly and add to the atmosphere of hope, love, and joy just like my predecessors, the Fezziwigs, taught me to do.

I thought I went to the meetings to stop using. To stop doing "it." I didn't know that abstinence was only the beginning of my recovery. I didn't know it was about learning how to live, love, and feel free. Free to be me. Free to let you be you. I am free to be exactly who my higher power made me to be. I am not ashamed of my personality. Orange is my favorite color.

My husband likes silver. People have preferences. I will not be everyone's cup of tea. We don't have to like every addict, but we must love them in a very special way.

So, let's love and be loved. Let's live and let live. My sponsor always reminds that the joy is in the journey. Let's welcome the suffering with open hearts. Let's celebrate life as the motley crew of survivors we are. I'm not saying we should shut off our good judgment. I look both ways before I cross the street, and then I make a decision about whether I should cross or not. Boundaries keep us safe. They require us to understand that there are consequences for our choices. Judgment is a far cry from being judgmental!

I have had to make decisions to love people from afar. I am sure I will be required to do so again. This does not give me license to feel superior to, gossip about, or punish another addict who is suffering because of active addiction—whether or not they are having a physical or emotional relapse—in any way, shape, or form. Someone else's suffering ought never be paraded around by those of us who claim to love unconditionally.

Unconditional love is an action. It is a state of being that holds a place of hope for those who are still suffering, regardless of clean time. Unconditional love is a practice. We will always fall short, but that will keep us humble. Humility, the posture of a beggar, as Charles Dickens spoke of it, is the ideal state for us to reside in. All of us, myself included, will fail each other from time to time. I thank God that we take turns being assholes in the rooms of twelve-step meetings. It's OK; it's all right. It's not about us; it's about the message. We carry it to the best of our ability, and by God, I am speaking the truth when I say *living* the steps in our own lives on a regular basis helps us do it well.

So, speak loud, speak softly, share regularly, open a meeting, sponsor someone, pour some coffee, hug a newcomer, cry with someone, share what is really going on with you, laugh with someone, or pray with someone. Guess what? We will do that, and we will recover. Every member's experience strength and hope matters. You may be the only message someone can hear. We never know.

Thank you, Fezziwigs! Thank you for doing the inside job. Thank you for interfering with the disease of addiction. Thank you for sharing your experience, strength, and hope!

I am light as a feather! I am grateful for the chance and hope I have been given.

CPSIA information can be obtained
at www.ICGtesting.com
Printed in the USA
LVHW091556010521
686193LV00004B/242